My pet

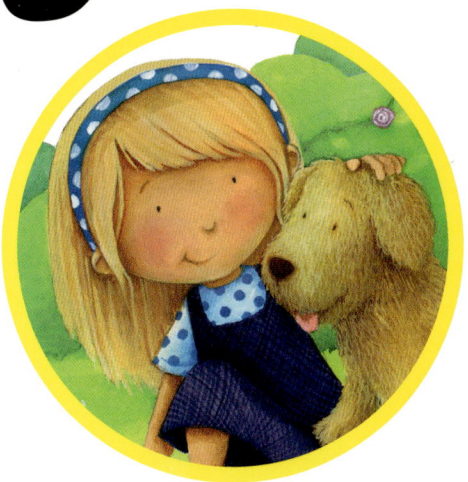

written by Jay Dale

illustrated by Kirsten Richards

Here is my fish.

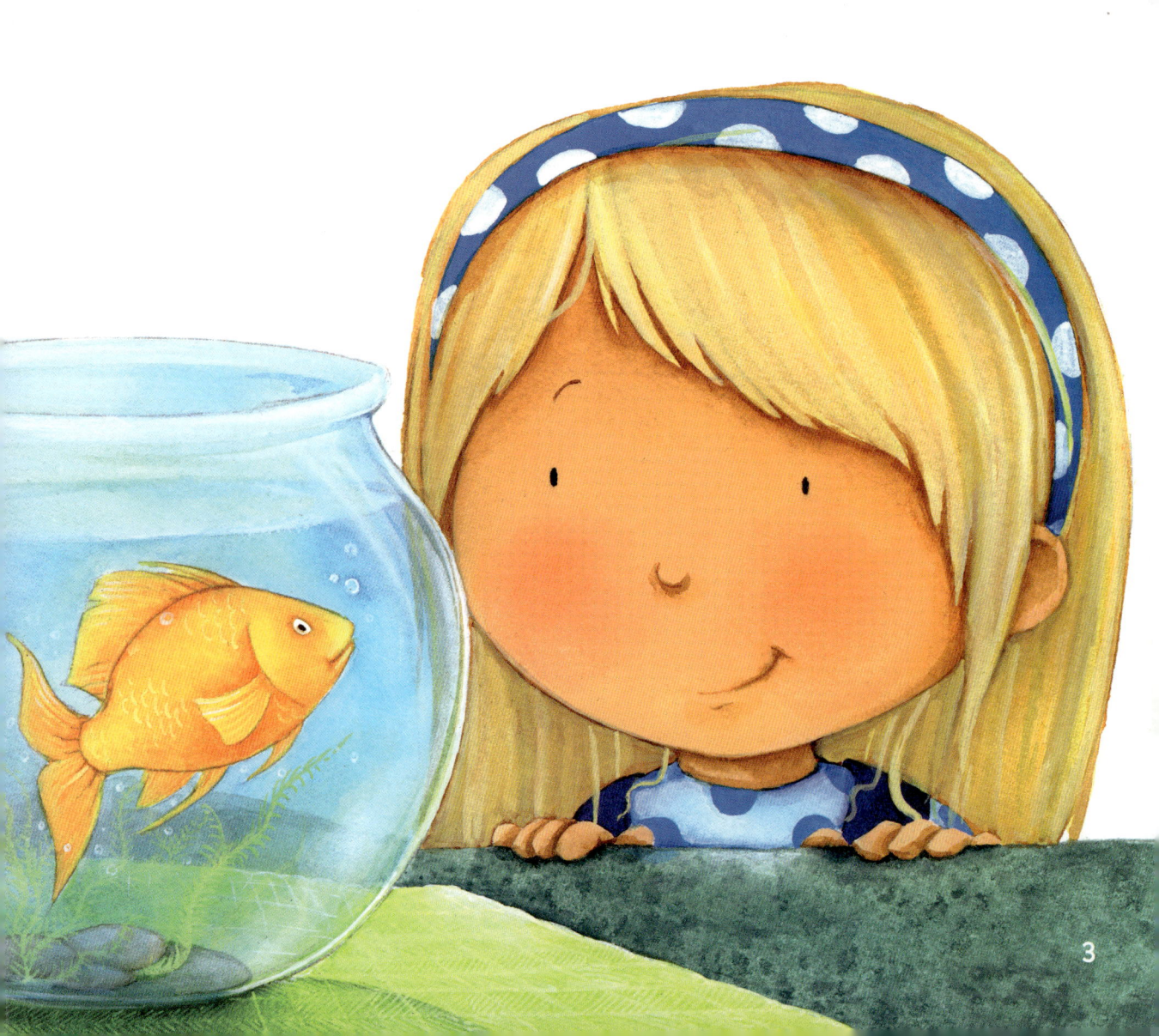

Here is my turtle.

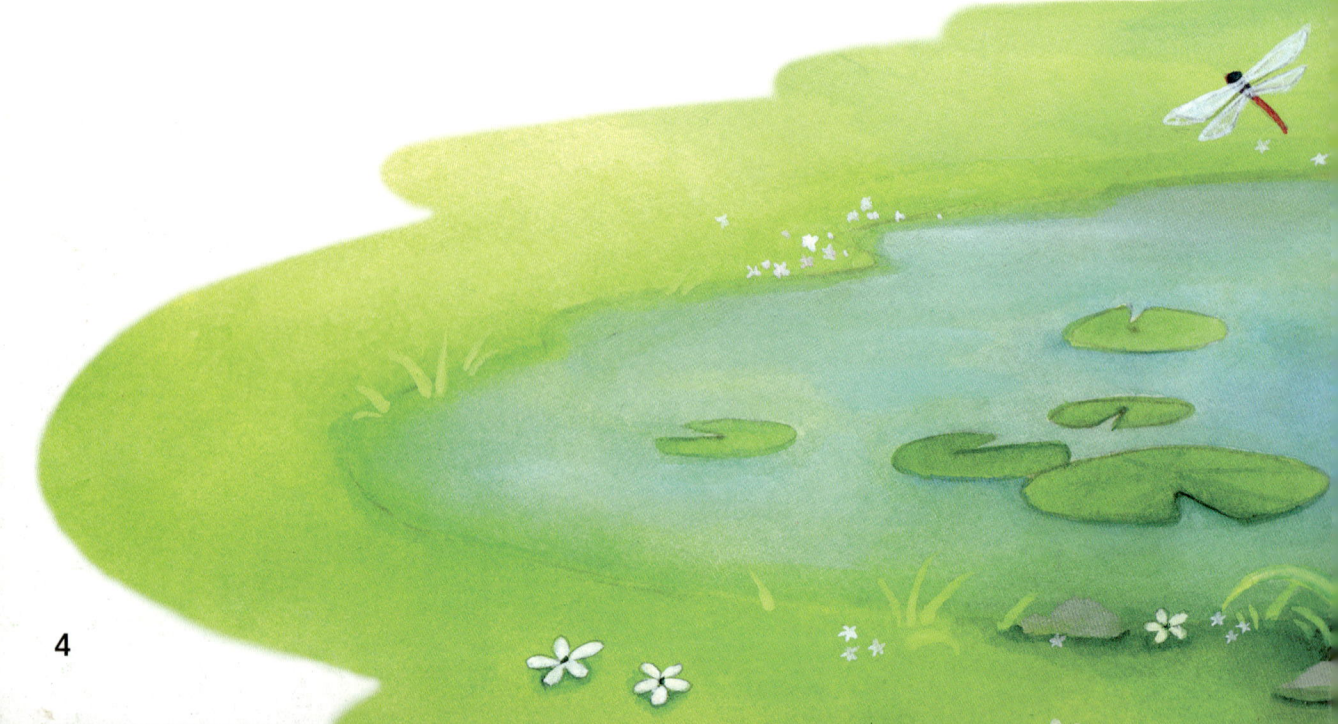

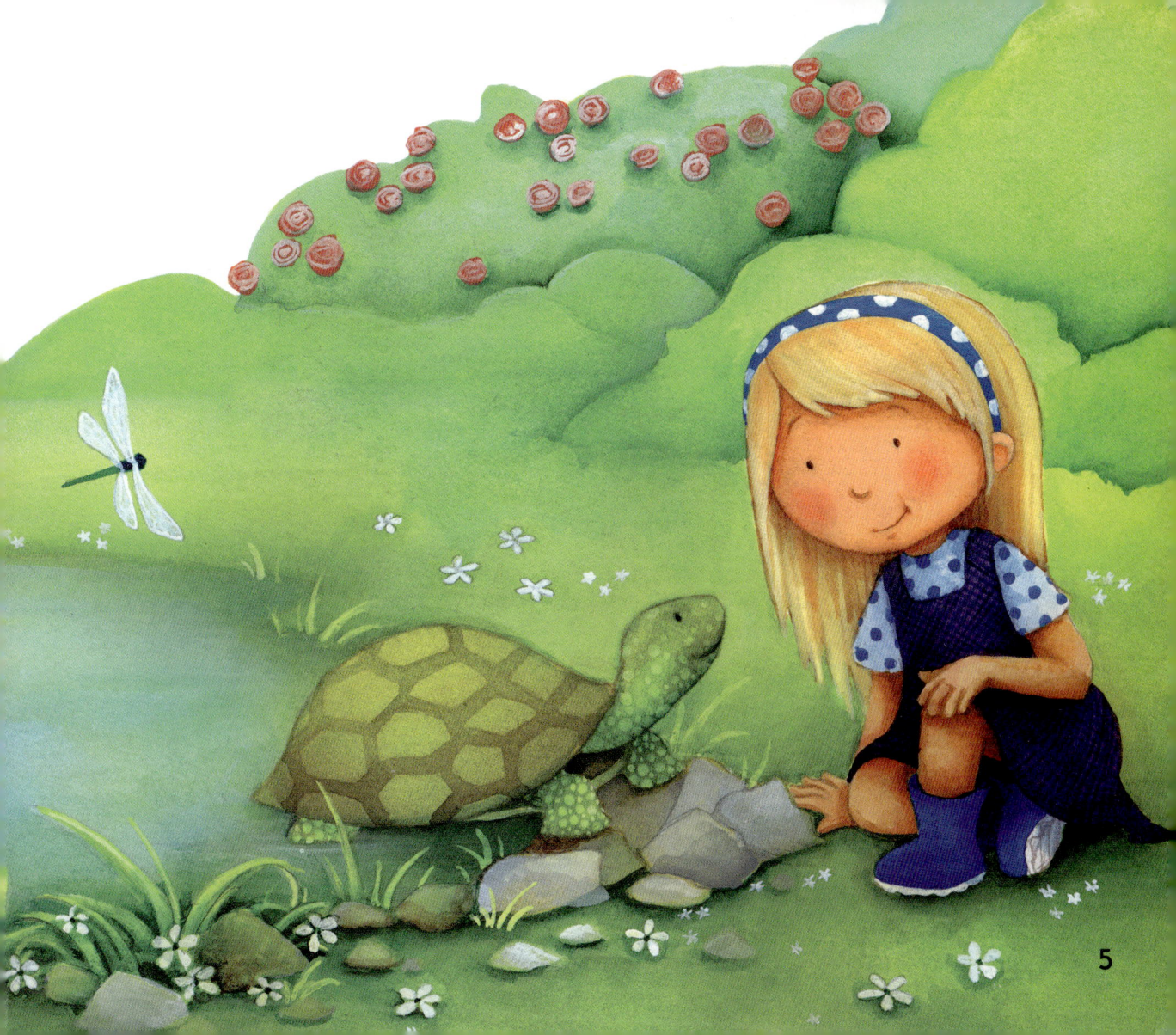

Here is my rabbit.

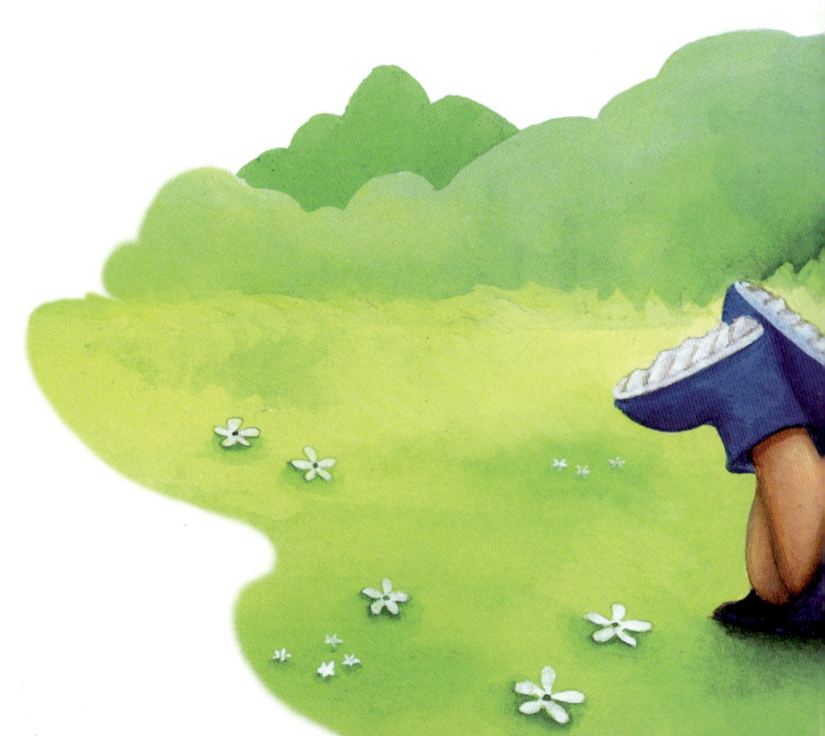

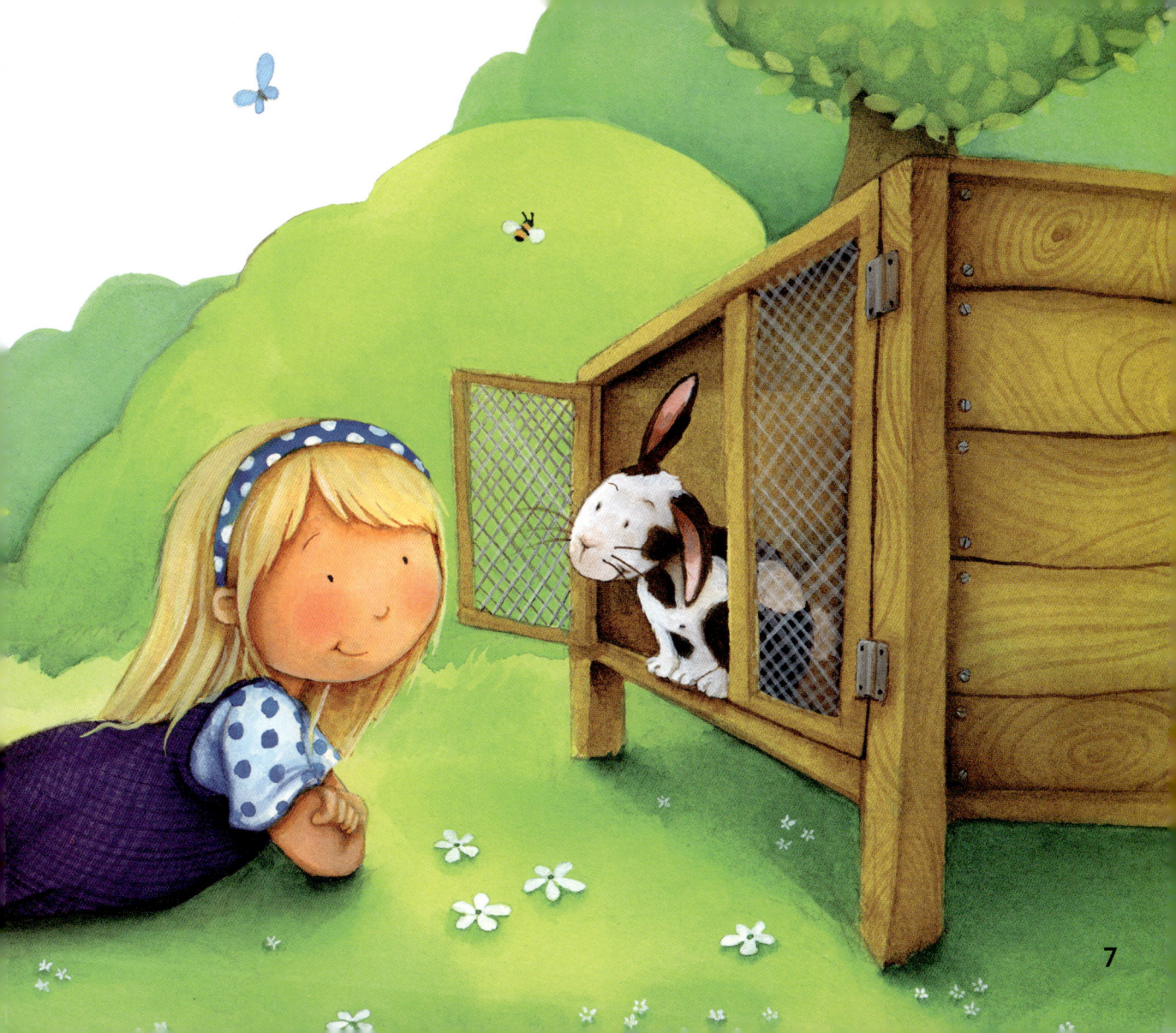

Here is my guinea pig.

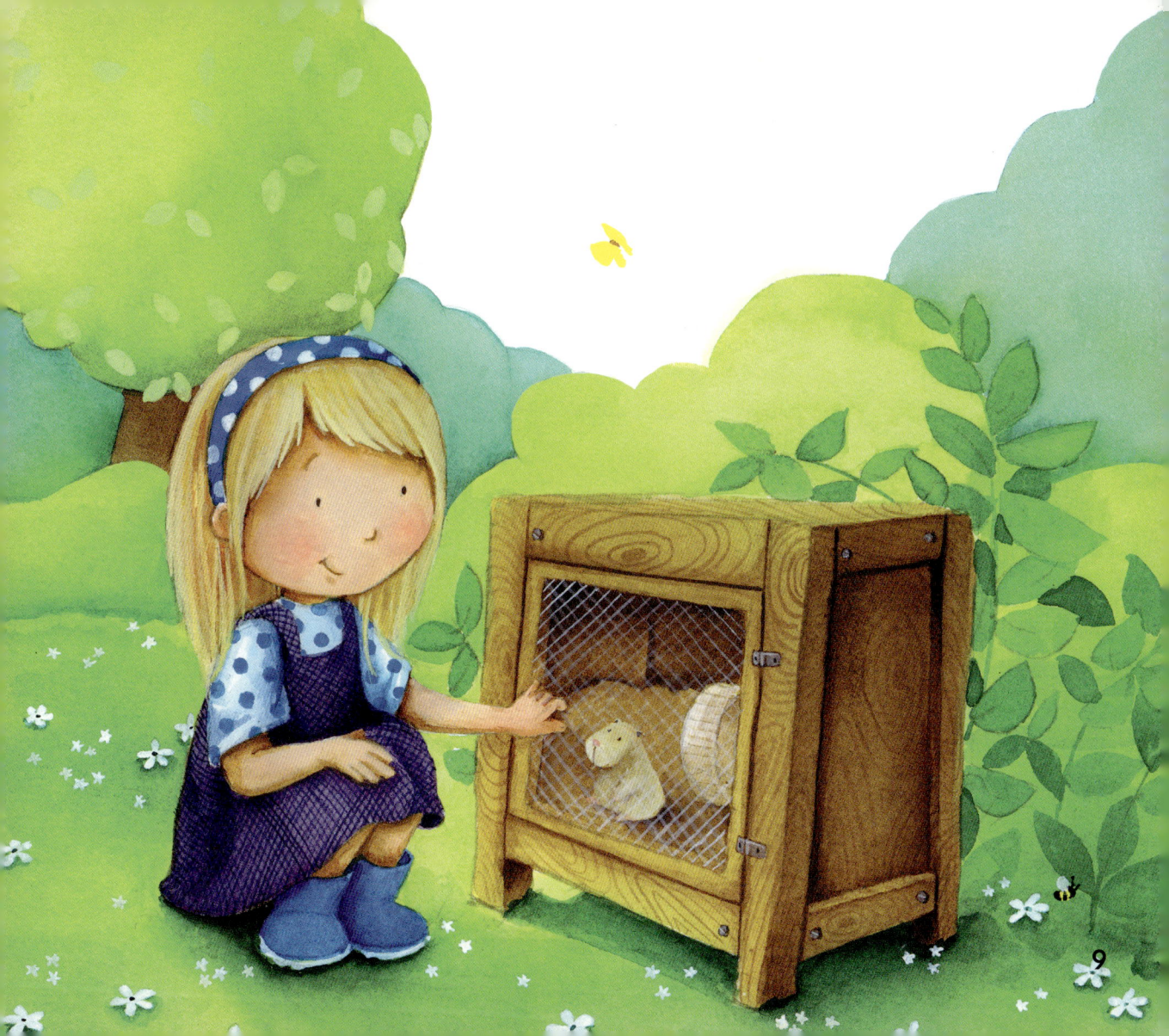

Here is my bird.

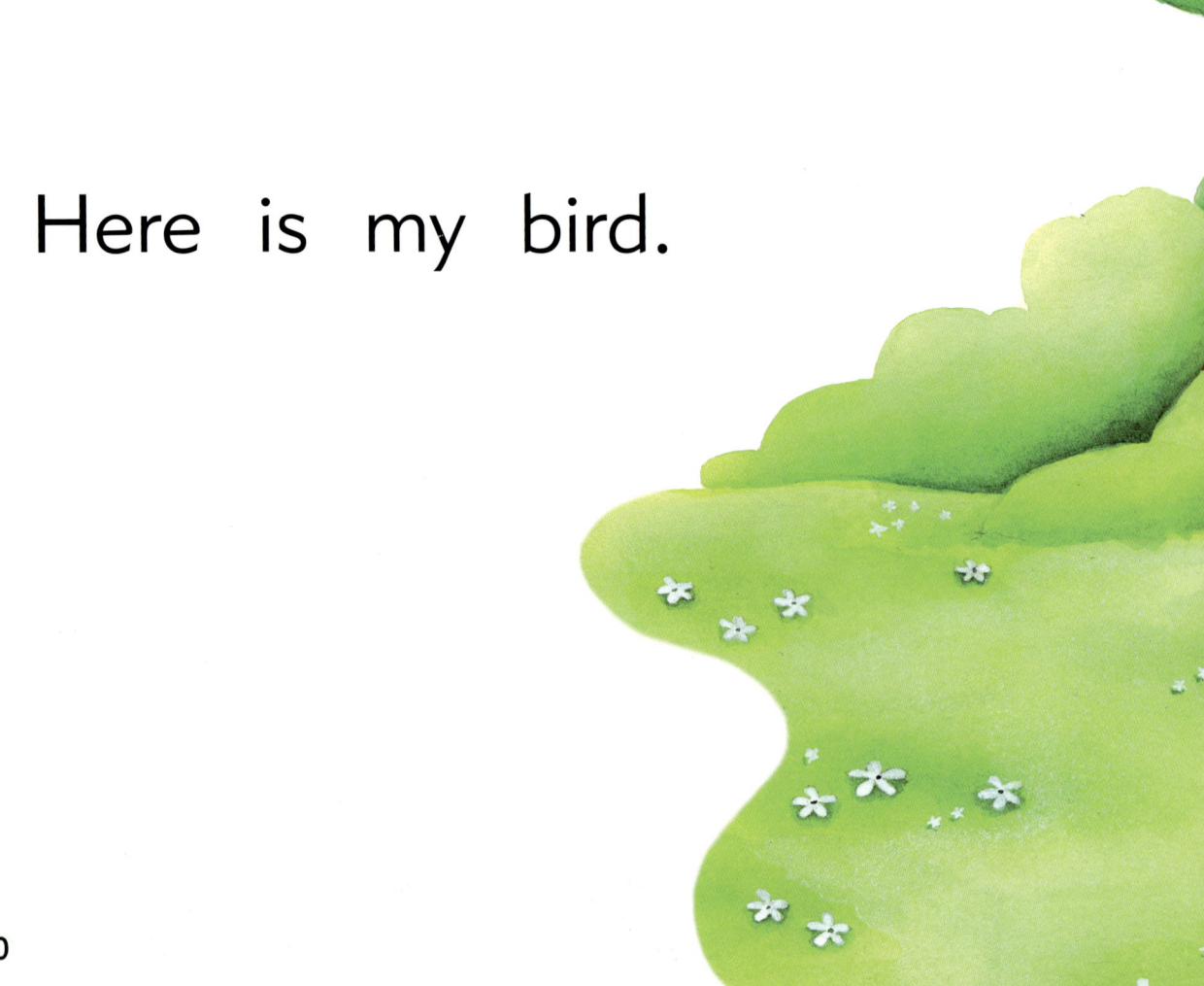

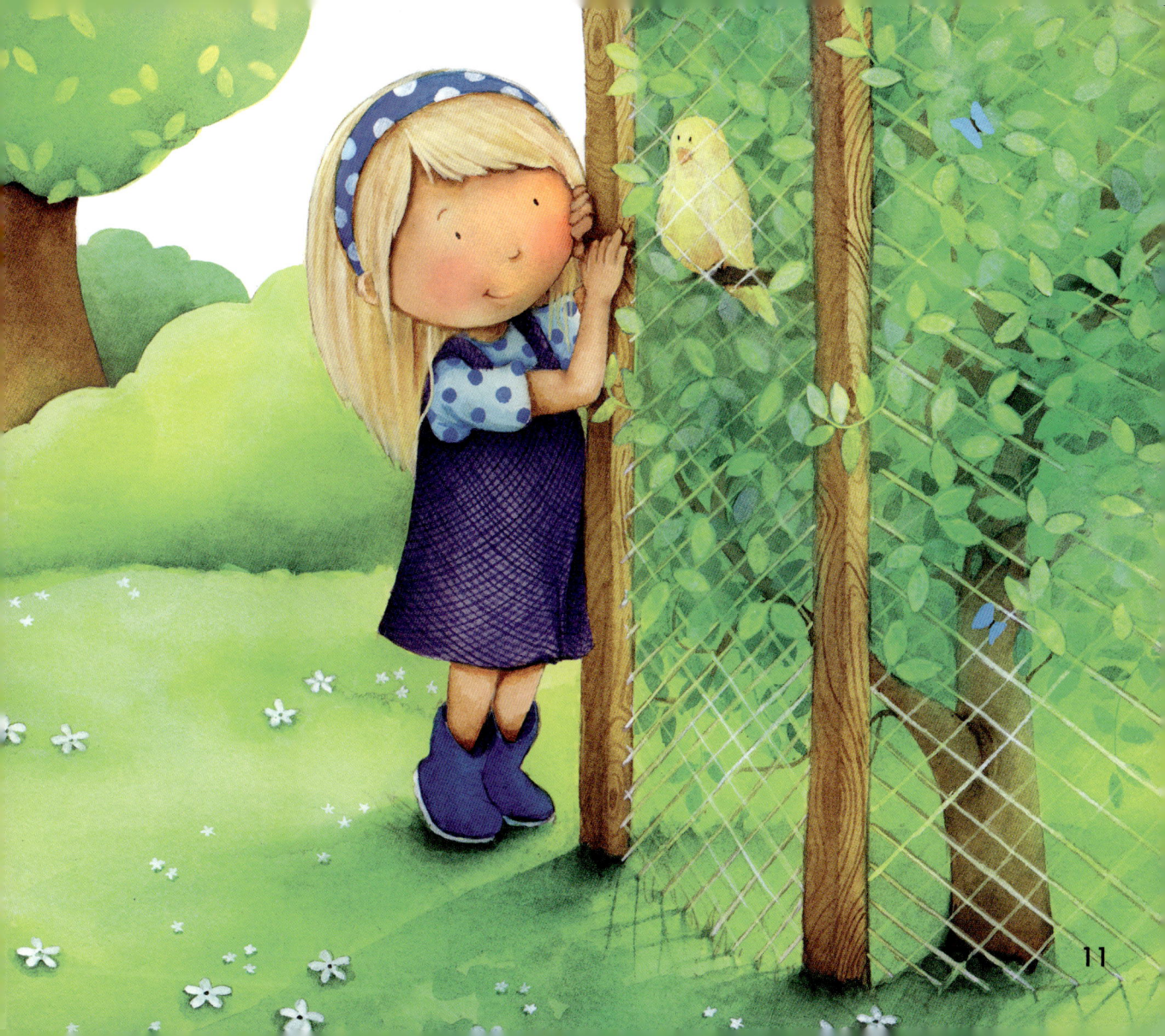

Here is my cat.

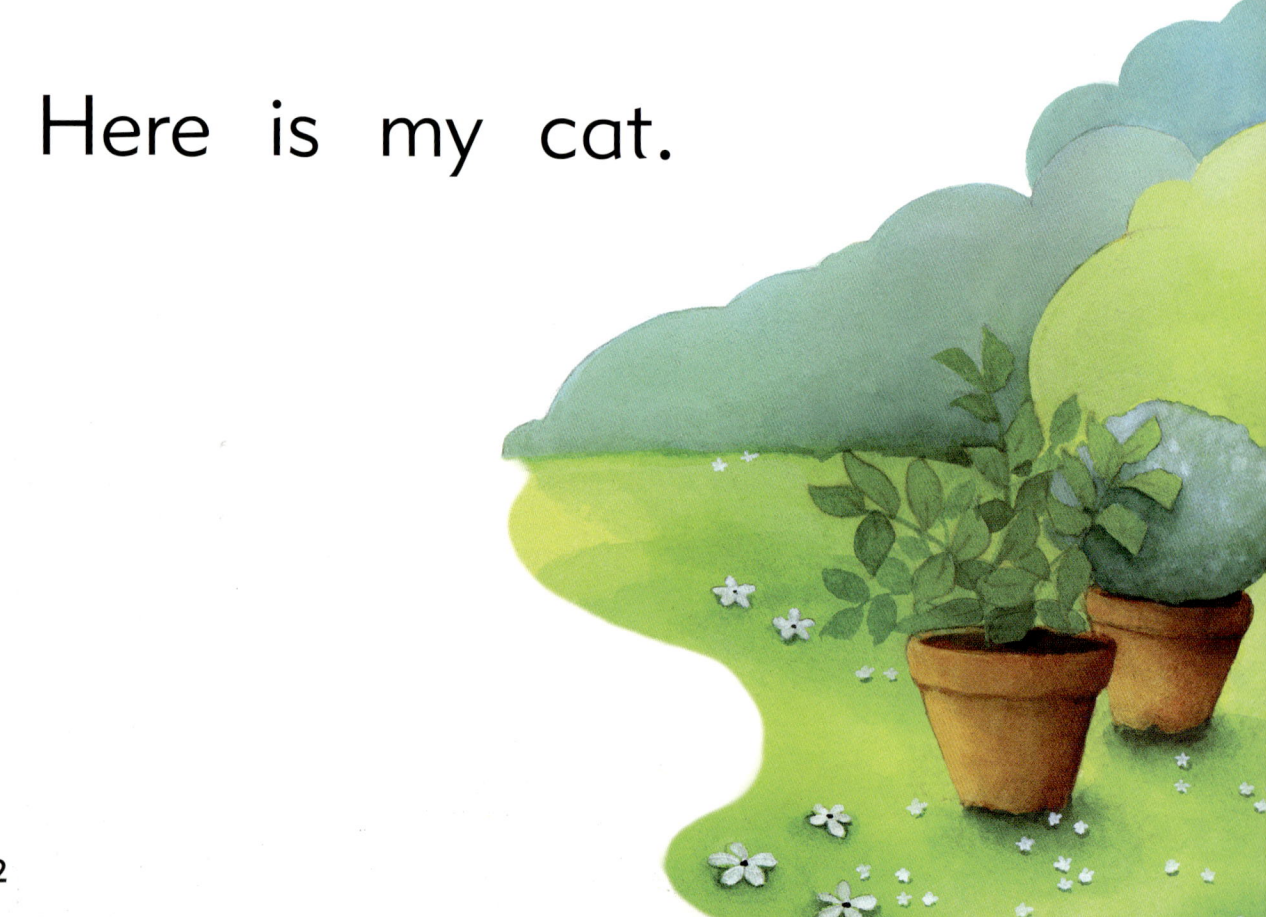

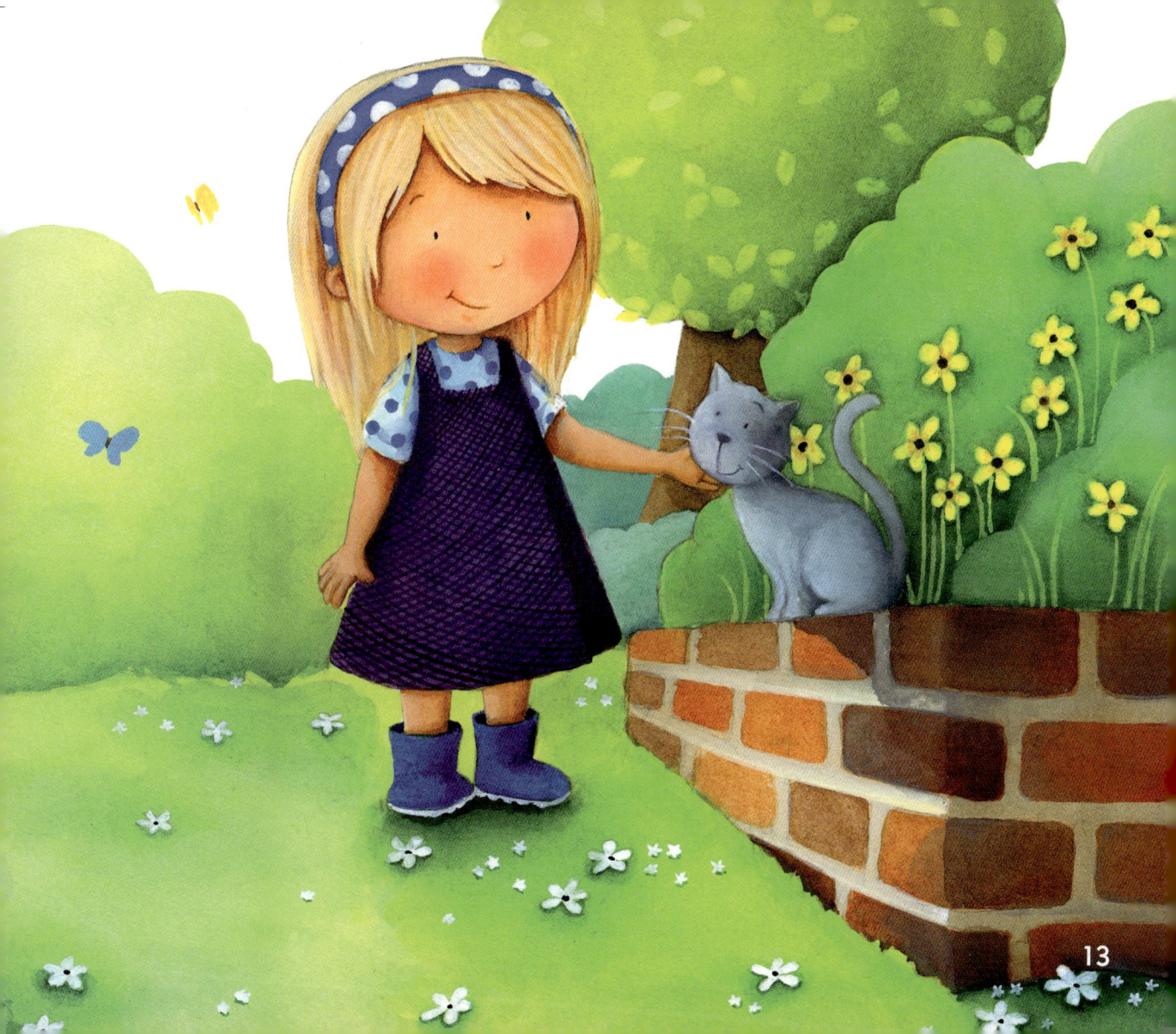

Here is my dog.

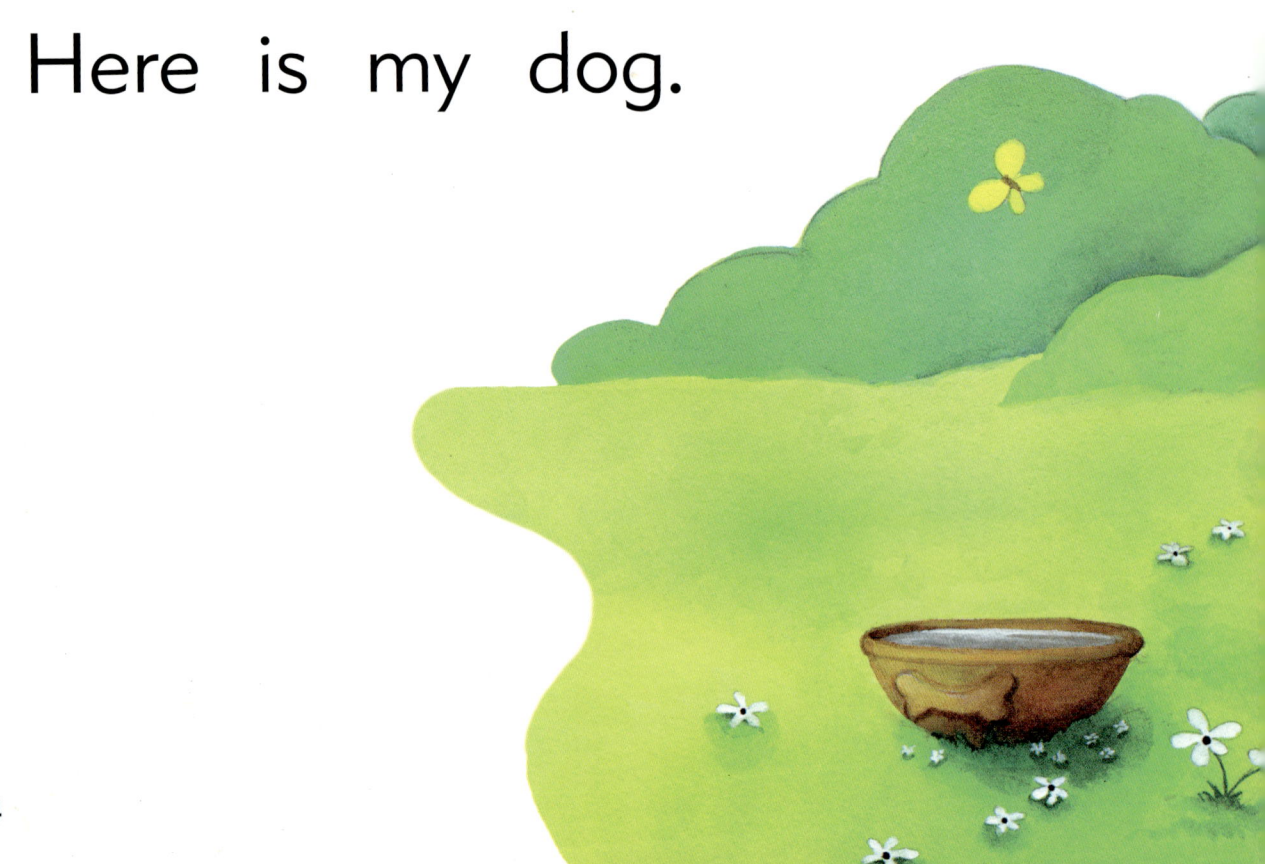

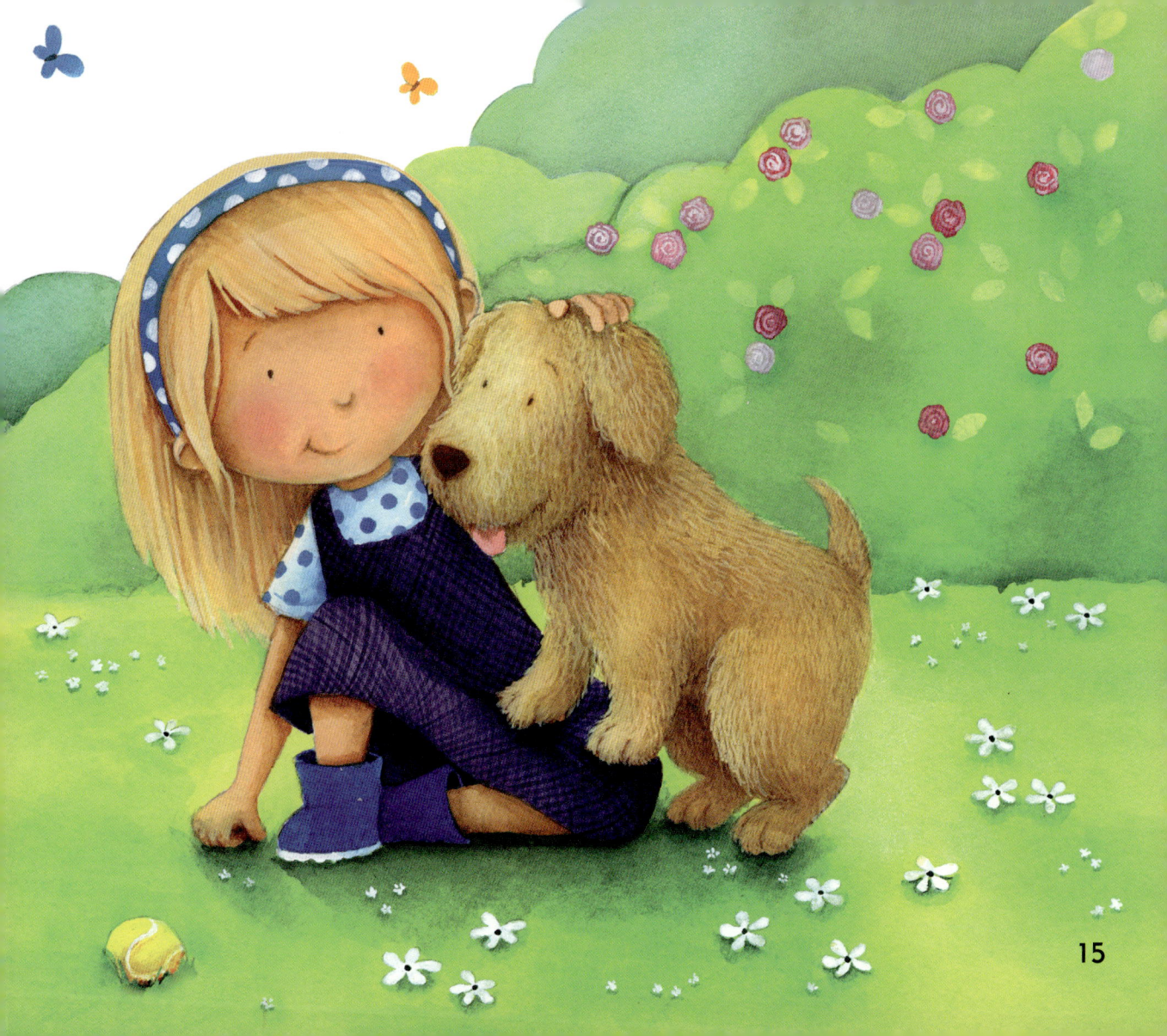

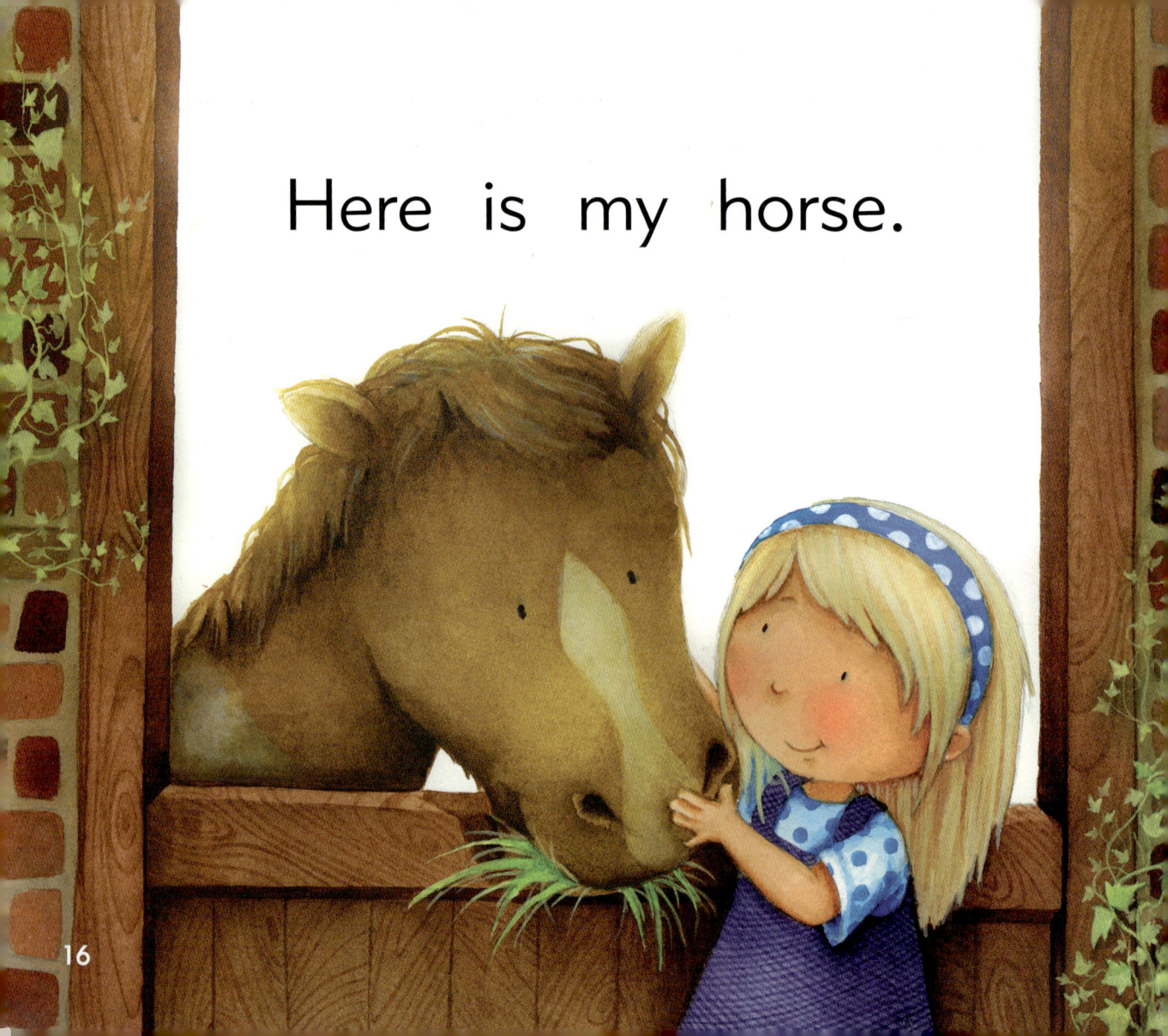
Here is my horse.